The ABC's of Answered Prayer

ISBN-10: 0615816770

ISBN-13: 978-0615816777

Gary Powers Publishing

Cover by Greg Brown

This book is dedicated to:

First and foremost to my heavenly Father God, my loving savior Jesus Christ, and the beloved Holy Spirit for entrusting me with this book and then to

All those who hunger and thirst for Righteousness. (Matthew 5:6)

And

To those who wish to enrich their prayer lives and their walk with The Lord.

Special Thanks

My most heartfelt and special thanks to Almighty God my Heavenly Father, my Lord and Savior Jesus Christ, and to the precious Holy Spirit for giving me this work and entrusting me with it and for their assistance in writing, publishing and distributing this book and getting it into your hands.

My heartfelt thanks go out to all those that assisted in various ways in preparation and completion of this book and for all those that prayed for the completion, distribution, and sale of the book.

Finally, special thanks to all that have purchased this book or have received it as a gift and read it.

Introduction

I was given the basic draft of "The ABC's of Answered Prayer" several years ago by the Spirit of God. This took only a very few minutes and "The ABC's of Answered Prayer" in its basic form was born.

There is scripture reference to everything listed alphabetically for answered prayer.

I primarily leaned toward the original King James Version of the Bible for the actual scriptural references. What I have written tells the main gist and meaning reflected in the scriptures. This is not quoting any particular version of the Bible but will agree with various versions of the Bible in regard to the meaning and message that is presented therein.

Some direct Bible quotes in the book are from the New King James Version of the Bible and are specially noted as such.

 I also quote the King James Version as KJV and at times will state see KJV without directly quoting the King James Bible in order to more clearly bring out the scriptural meaning referenced in the text.

It is my sincerest desire that this book will be a blessing to the reader. I hope it will enrich their lives, increase their knowledge of God's Word, ultimately will enhance their prayer life, and strengthen their relationship with the Lord Jesus Christ.

Sincerely,

Gary Powers

3rd John 2nd Verse

Ist Corinthians 13th Chapter

Psalm 37:5

Table of Contents

THE ABC'S OF ANSWERED PRAYER

(A – C)

A. **Ask:** Ask so that you may receive; (Matthew 7: 7-11) & (Luke 11:9 -10) "...you do not have because you do not ask." (James 4:2b NKJV™)

B. **Believe:** Jesus said, "And all things, whatever things you ask in prayer, believing, you will receive." (Matthew 21:22 NKJV™) Also see Mark 9:23.

C. **Confess:** Confess the Word of God when you pray because God's Word is His will. Scripture tells us: "Now this is the confidence that we have in Him, that if we ask anything according to His will, He hears us. And if we know that He hears us, whatever we ask, we know that we have the petitions that we have asked of Him." (1st John 5:14-15 NKJV™)

(D-G)

D. **Do not doubt.** It is important that we pray in faith and **do not doubt** but believe that we will receive what we are praying for. (Mark 11:23) & (James 1: 5 - 7)

E. **Every day give thanks**. (Ephesians 5:20) & (Philippians 4:6) **every day** when you pray we should do what scripture says and "Enter into His gates with thanksgiving…" (Psalm 100:4a KJV)

F. **Forgive:** We are to **forgive** others before we pray. If we don't forgive other people, our Heavenly Father won't forgive us (Mark 11:25 & 26) and this will hinder our prayers.

G. **Go forward**. Look at the story where Jesus talks about the Centurion and notice how Jesus told him to go his way as he had believed it would be done for him. (Mathew 8:5-13) When we pray we need to receive the answer by faith. The bible defines faith in the present or in the now as follows: "Now faith is the substance of things hoped for, the evidence of things not seen." (Hebrews 11:1 KJV) As we receive what we are praying for in faith our faith will have a substance of what we do not see at that time, yet it is something real and tangible in the spirit realm, and if we continue to believe doing our part and not doubt, it will materialize in accordance with God's will and in His perfect timing. So actually we really do **go forward** by believing it has happened in the faith realm and that we will get what we are praying for in the natural realm.

(H-I)

H. **Hallow** the name of the Lord. When we hallow something it is to consider it sacred or holy. In the Lord's Prayer Jesus taught us when we pray to **hallow** our heavenly Father's name; in other words, we are to look at his name as sacred. Jesus said, "In this manner, therefore, pray: Our Father in heaven, Hallowed be Your name." (Mathew 6:9 NKJV™) We can go on to praise and worship His name. You can **hallow** the names of Jehovah; Jehovah Rapha means the Lord our Healer for healing; Jehovah Jireh, which means The Lord our provider, for provision, etc.

I. **Inquire** as to God's specific will in your situation, from His Word. God's word is His will for us. I once had a friend that said that the word

BIBLE stood for the following: **B**asic **I**nstructions **B**efore **L**eaving **E**arth. Scripture shows that we are to study to show ourselves approved unto God as a workman.... rightly dividing the word of truth. (2nd Timothy 2:15 see KJV) The word of truth spoken of here is God's word (John 17:17) and we know God's word is His will. As mentioned earlier above under **C Confess**, if we **inquire** into God's word and find a promise concerning our request and find out what God's word says about what we are asking, it places us in position to receive the answer to our prayer. Note that there are over 3,000 promises contained in God's word and we can claim those that apply to our need or situation that we are praying for.

(J-L)

J. **Jesus** is the answer and He is the way. Pray to the Father in **Jesus'** name. Jesus said in his word "I am the way, the truth, and the life. No one comes to the Father except through me." (John 14:6 NKJV™) **Jesus** also said, "And whatever you ask in My name, that I will do, that the Father may be glorified in the Son. If you ask anything in My name, I will do it."
(John 14:13 & 14 NKJV™)

K. **Know** God hears you if pray according to his will. Remember "...he who comes to God must believe that He is, and *that* He is a rewarder of those who diligently seek Him." (Hebrews 11:6 NKJV™) Also see 1st John 5:14-15.

L. **Love and grow in love** (1st John 4:7), "for God is love..."

(1st John 4:8b NKJV™) In 1st Corinthians the 13th chapter the whole chapter is devoted to **love**. Jesus commanded us to love. (John 13: 34) & (John 15:12)

M. **Move toward the answer**, step out in faith. The bible tells us that one night Jesus was walking on the water and Peter saw him and asked him; if it is You, command me to come to You, so Jesus told him to come. Peter then stepped out of the boat in faith and obedience to the Lord and started to walk on the water, walking toward Jesus. He did all right until he saw that the wind was blowing hard and he took his eyes off of Jesus and looked at the situation around him and then he started to sink. Just as he started to sink, he cried out to Jesus and asked him to save him. Immediately Jesus stretched out his hand and rescued him. (Matthew 14:25-33) The point here is that Peter stepped out in faith and moved toward Jesus, and as long as he kept his eyes on Jesus, he was victorious, but when he looked at the circumstances surrounding him, it was then that he lost his victory and began to sink. Peter would have never walked on water had he not stepped out in faith. Sometimes faith is simply acting on information received from God and **moving toward the answer**.

N. **Never give up**. Remember Abraham – have bulldog tenacity. Abraham's name was originally Abram, and God changed his name to Abraham meaning "father of

Many nations." (Genesis 17:5) When Abram had no children, God promised him that his future descendants would be so great that they would be as many as the stars in the sky. (Genesis 15:5) & (Hebrews 11: 8 - 12) Abram did not even have his first child, Ishmael, until he was 86 years old. (Genesis 16:16) God told Abraham when he was 99 years old and only had one son that he would be a father of many nations. (Genesis 17: 1 & 4) God told Abraham He would give him another son named Isaac by his wife Sarah, who was then 90 years old, and Abraham would be 100 years old by the time Isaac would be born. (Genesis 17:17) Abraham was an old man and Sarah was well past child-bearing years and it looked impossible but he **never gave up.** Even under these circumstances Abraham believed God. Scripture tells us "… Abraham believed God, and it was counted unto him for righteousness." (Romans 4:3 See KJV) If you belong to Christ, you are part of Abraham's seed and one of his descendants. (Galatians 3:29)

O. **Open your heart.** Jesus stands at the door of our heart and knocks, open it to him and let him in. (Revelation 3:20) Next **Open** your eyes and ears (Matthew 13:16) look for the answer to your prayer and listen to your heart and to what the scriptures say about what you are praying for. **Open** your eyes and see yourself receiving the answer by believing and by having faith. (Mark 11:24)

P. **Praise** the Lord, "Enter into his gates

with thanksgiving, *And* into His courts with praise:" (Psalm 100:4a KJV) **Praise** Him for the answer before it comes for this shows Him that you have faith and that you believe for what you are praying for. (Matthew 21:22)

Q. **Quit murmuring and complaining**. (Philippians 2:14) Don't talk the problem, talk the solution. Find a promise in the Bible, stand on it and say what God says on the subject.

R. **Release your faith** -- let go and let God. Jesus said "Have faith in God." (Mark 11:22b KJV) Also see 1st Peter 5:6 & 7.

S. **Stand on the Word of God**. Heaven and earth will pass away, but God's Word will never pass away. (Mark 13:31) The Bible is God's Word, and if we are praying according to His Word or one of His promises in His Word, we can **stand** firm on it and know that "God is not a man, that He should lie;..." (Numbers 23: 19a KJV) Know God's word is more real than what we see, feel, touch, taste, or experience.

T. **Thank God for the answer.** (Ephesians 5:20) & (Philippians 4:6) Scripture says "in everything give thanks; for this is the will of God in Christ Jesus for you." (1st Thessalonians 5:18 NKJV™) When we pray and ask God for something and **thank him** in advance we are praying in faith and faith moves God.

U. **Understand** that it may take some time and happen in a way least expected. We must **understand** that God's thoughts are not our thoughts and His ways are not our ways because His ways and thoughts are higher than ours. (Isaiah 55:8 & 9)

V. **Victoriously** receive the answer. The bible says that God always causes us to triumph in Christ (2nd Corinthians 2:14) and "...we are more than conquerors through him that loved us." (Romans 8:37 KJV) These are reasons for us to be **victorious**.

W. **Work** and do your part -- "...faith without works is dead" (James 2:20b KJV) There is an old saying of Benjamin Franklin that goes like this, "God helps those that help themselves." Though this is not found in the Bible, there is some truth to this saying especially when we consider the previous scripture.

X. **"X"** out time every day to spend in prayer. Give the Lord the first part of your day, even if it is only a few minutes to dedicate your life anew and afresh to Him, giving Him thanksgiving and praise. David was a man after God's own heart (Acts 13:22) and he said, "O God, You are my God; Early will I seek You;" (Psalm 63:1a NKJV™). We should daily seek the Lord. (Isaiah 58:2) Make specific time for the Lord. We make appointments for everything else; why not make an appointed time for the Lord? After all, he should come first.

Y. **Yearn** for God and the answer and pray with your whole heart. Jesus told us that what things so ever we desire when we pray, that we should believe that we receive them, and we shall have them. (Mark 11:24 See KJV) Scripture tells us "He satisfies the longing soul, and fills the hungry soul with goodness." (Psalm 107:9 NKJV™)

Z. **Zeal: Pray with zeal.** The dictionary defines zeal as eager desire or endeavor, enthusiastic diligence. The Apostle Paul said, "But it is good to be zealously affected always in a good thing,..." (Galatians 4:18 KJV) and prayer is definitely a good thing. We should pray with earnest expectation and **zeal**.

Prayer for Salvation

If you want to accept Jesus Christ as your savior, become a child of God, and have eternal life pray the following prayer. Should you want scriptural references for it, you will find the prayer with the references included on page 19 under the heading "Prayer for Salvation with Scripture References."

O God, I come before You in the name of Jesus Christ. I believe that Jesus came in the flesh and was Your only begotten son. I also believe that He suffered and died on the cross for my sins and that He rose from the dead. I confess that I am a sinner and I ask that You forgive me of my sins and wash me in the blood of Jesus Christ. Jesus, I ask You to come into my heart, save me, and be the Lord of my life. Jesus, I now want to live for You. O God, You are now more than my God; You are my Heavenly Father and I am

Your child. Jesus, I will serve You all the days of my life and live for You and I thank You that You have given me everlasting life and that You came that I might have life and have it more abundantly. Jesus, I now receive You as my savior and the abundant life have blessed me with. Thank You Heavenly Father and Jesus Christ.

Amen.

If you prayed that prayer and meant it, you are now born again into the family of God. It is important that you tell someone what you have done and confess Jesus Christ as your Lord (Romans 10:9) because confession is made unto salvation. (Romans 10:10) Now you have over 3,000 promises given to you in the Bible, so I suggest you start reading your Bible and learning those promises and see how you can live a better, happier and more abundant life. It is also important that you find a good church that teaches the Bible, get baptized, and start going to church and Sunday school so you can learn about all the good things life now has to offer you as a Christian. You can now have a better life on earth, and someday you will go to heaven and live a wonderful life with God and Jesus forever.

Prayer for Salvation with Scripture References

Though the prayer is short, here are some scriptural references given and they are just a few of what could be given.

O God, I come before You in the name of Jesus Christ. (John 14:6, 13 & 14) I believe that Jesus came in the flesh (Galatians 4:4) & (1st John 4:2) and was your only begotten son. (Matthew 3:16 & 17), (John 3:16), & (1st John 4:9), I also believe that He suffered and died on the cross for my sins and that He rose from the dead. (Acts 17:3) & (Romans 4:24) I confess that I am a sinner (Romans 3:23) and I ask that You forgive me of my sins (1st John 1:9) and wash me in the blood of Jesus Christ. (Revelation 1:5) Jesus, I ask You to come into my heart, (Ephesians 3:17) save me, (Acts 16:31) & (Romans 10:9, 10 &13) and be the Lord of my life. Jesus, I now want to live for You. (2nd Corinthians 5:15) O God, You are now more than my God; You are my Heavenly Father and I am Your child. (John 1:12) & (Ephesians 1:5) Jesus, I will serve You all the days of my life and live for You (1st John 4:9) and I thank You that You have given me everlasting life (John 3:16) and that You came that I might have life and have it more abundantly. (John10:10) Jesus, I now receive You as my savior and the abundant life you have blessed me with. Thank You Heavenly Father and Jesus Christ.

Amen.

www.ingramcontent.com/pod-product-compliance
Lightning Source LLC
LaVergne TN
LVHW010550100826
845148LV00013B/2678